Nutrition For

CW00632035

NUTRITION

FOR

Teeth & Bones

•

LAURA GRANGER, MPH, RD
AND THE HEALTH MEDIA
EDITORIAL PANEL

foulsham
LONDON • NEW YORK • TORONTO •
SYDNEY

foulsham
Yeovil Road, Slough, Berkshire SL1 4JH

ISBN 0–572–01717–0

Copyright © Slawson Communications Inc. 1992

This British Edition © W. Foulsham & Co Ltd

Printed in Great Britain by
St Edmundsbury Press Ltd, Bury St Edmunds, Suffolk.

Contents

Introduction

Many people have realised that the familiar instruction from childhood, "Drink your milk," was possibly some of the best health advice they ever received. Calcium, a mineral found in milk and other low-fat dairy products, is linked with the prevention and treatment of numerous diseases including osteoporosis, high blood pressure (hypertension), cardiovascular disease, and cancer.

Many questions remain for the consumer attempting to choose a diet and adopt a lifestyle that prevents these diseases. Many individuals want to know if they are at risk of developing a diet-related disease.

As people live longer, diseases such as osteoporosis that affect the older population are receiving increasing attention. Evidence suggests that there are ways an individual might be protected from developing osteoporosis and other degenerative diseases.

NUTRITION FOR TEETH & BONES provides information on the functions of calcium, the best dietary and supplemental sources of the mineral, how much calcium is recommended to prevent disease, why a calcium deficiency can cause osteoporosis or other disorders, and the possible effects of calcium overdose.

1
Are We Getting Enough Calcium?

How Much Calcium Do People Need?

The daily calcium requirement varies and depends on age, sex, and physiological state. The current recommended dietary allowance for adults is 500 mg of calcium daily. Children from 11 to 18 years old as well as pregnant or breastfeeding women need 1,200 mg per day. For infants up to a year old calcium needs are calculated based on body weight. An intake of 60 mg per kg (1 kg = 2.2 lb) of body weight is recommended. This means that an infant weighing 6 kg (13 lb) should consume 360 mg of calcium daily, or the amount of calcium in 1¼ cups of milk. These advised levels take into account that only about 30% of the calcium in foods will be absorbed by the body. (*Graph 1, Page 12*)

The allowances are revised every few years as nutrition research provides new

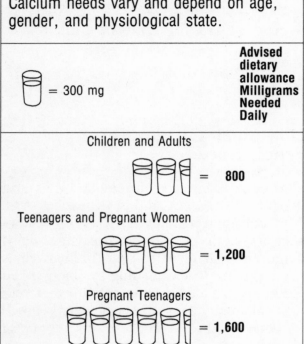

Graph 1.
Calcium needs vary and depend on age, gender, and physiological state.

= 300 mg

Advised dietary allowance Milligrams Needed Daily

Children and Adults

= 800

Teenagers and Pregnant Women

= 1,200

Pregnant Teenagers

= 1,600

information. The adult daily allowance for calcium may perhaps increase to 1,000 mg because of evidence that shows a daily intake of 500 mg might not be adequate to prevent or treat osteoporosis. The best intake to prevent degenerative diseases is not known. Some researchers suggest that 1,000 mg of calcium is not enough and that 1,500 mg of calcium is required to prevent age-related bone loss and osteoporosis.

The Calcium Content Of The Average Diet

A low calcium diet is common. Several national nutrition surveys examined the adequacy of diets and found them to be inadequate in calcium.

In particular, women, older adults, and teenagers are at risk for calcium deficiency. Daily consumption of calcium is less than half of the advised dietary allowance in those who do not drink milk. (*Graph 2, Below*)

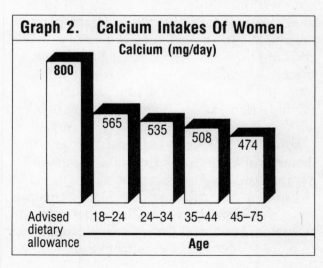

Graph 2.   Calcium Intakes Of Women

Calcium (mg/day)

800

565

535

508

474

Advised dietary allowance | 18–24 | 24–34 | 35–44 | 45–75

Age

Males do better than females with an average estimated calcium intake of 700 mg/day. Intake is usually higher during adolescence and is lowest for men 50 years old or older. For females, the average intake is only 450 mg/day. Dietary intake decreases with age; women 35 years old or older have the lowest intake of calcium.

There are several reasons why people are not getting enough calcium.

Reduced Consumption Of Low-Fat Dairy Foods: Low-fat dairy foods, such as milk, yogurt, cheese, and cottage cheese can provide three-quarters of the daily intake of calcium. In contrast, fatty dairy foods, such as sour cream, cream cheese, cream, and butter supply little or no calcium. Limited intake of low-fat dairy foods might place a person at risk of calcium deficiency. Milk consumption has decreased and calcium is usually low in the diets of girls and women. One of the causes for this reduction in calcium-rich milk might be soft drinks. The decrease in calcium and increase in phosphorus intakes that result from this dietary substitution might place a person at high risk of calcium deficiency.

Lactose Intolerance: Many people consume few dairy products because of an inability to digest these foods. Intolerance of dairy foods often stems from a deficiency of the enzyme, lactase. Lactase is needed for the body to digest the milk sugar called lactose. Without lactase, undigested sugar remains in the intestine and is consumed by bacteria that naturally inhabit this area. Symptoms such as gas, bloating, and diarrhoea can result. A higher incidence of lactose intolerance is found in people with osteoporosis than in healthy people. This finding supports the theory that inability to consume dairy products might be significant in causing osteoporosis.

Weight Control Diets: A diet that provides 1,600 calories or less might not supply adequate amounts of calcium. Many weight-watchers are women for whom an adequate calcium intake is important. Chronic dieters are a high risk group for calcium deficiency as well as marginal or low intakes of other nutrients.

Misconceptions About Calcium Needs: Misinformation about calcium needs throughout life can result in inadequate intake of calcium. Many people think that calcium is necessary only during the growing years and that milk and high calcium intakes are not needed once bones are formed. This is not true. Bones are continually reformed throughout life. About 320 mg of calcium are excreted from the body every day, regardless of the dietary intake.

If the dietary intake of calcium does not replace the daily losses, a calcium deficit results and calcium is lost from the bone. In time a chronic gradual loss of calcium can result in osteoporosis.

Dietary Sources Of Calcium

Dairy products are the best sources of calcium. Low-fat milk and yogurt (35% of the calories come from fat) or nonfat milk and yogurt (less than 0.5% fat calories), and low-fat hard cheeses are the most concentrated sources of calcium (*Figure 1, Opposite*). Ice cream, whole milk (50% fat calories), cottage cheese, and cheeses like cheddar provide calcium, but are high in fat. Non-dairy foods such as tinned fish (with bones), oranges, tofu (soybean curd), and dark green leafy vegetables also contribute to calcium intake. Because of the oxalates in dark green leafy vegetables, these foods might not provide as much usable calcium as low-fat dairy sources. Oxalates are substances in foods that bind to calcium in the intestine and reduce its absorption.

A 250 ml/8 fl oz/1 cup serving of low-fat milk or yogurt, or a 40 g/1½ oz/3 tbsp serving of low-fat hard cheese contains about 300 mg

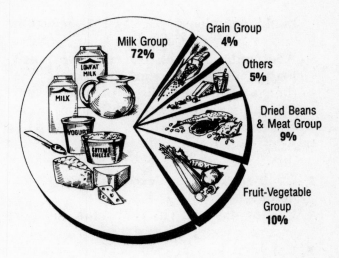

Figure 1.   Dietary Contributors To Calcium Intake

of calcium. To include at least 800 mg of calcium in the diet each day a person should consume at least two servings of milk, yogurt, or cheese. The additional calcium needs can be met by other foods in the diet. Those people who tolerate milk but prefer not to drink it might try the following techniques to increase their calcium intake.

• Add nonfat dry milk powder to casseroles and cheese sauces. One tablespoon of nonfat dry milk supplies 52 mg of calcium and only 15 calories.

- Add nonfat dry milk to recipes for french toast, milkshakes, dips, puddings, pie fillings, homemade breads, and mashed potatoes (2 tablespoons to every one cup of potatoes).
- Add nonfat dry milk to creamy salad dressings.
- Cook rice and hot cereal in low-fat or nonfat milk.
- Use low-fat yogurt as a substitute for sour cream in recipes.
- Combine low-fat milk with nonfat dry milk solids and use instead of cream in soups and sauces.
- Use low-fat cheeses with fruit and crackers for snacks.
- Include several servings of calcium-rich vegetables in the daily diet.

People who cannot tolerate milk must plan their diets carefully to include an adequate amount of calcium. Meat, chicken, and fresh or frozen fish are poor sources of calcium. At least three servings each day must be included in the diet to ensure adequate intake. In addition, a person must receive frequent exposure to sunlight or a supplement of vitamin D to ensure calcium absorption.

Milk should not be eliminated from the diets of small children unless recommended by a doctor. Children have small stomachs and a limited capacity for food. It is unlikely they can consume enough calcium on a diet without milk products because of the increased quantity of food that must be consumed. One good source of non-dairy calcium is fortified soy milk.

2
Calcium: The Basics

What Is Calcium?

Calcium is a mineral found in abundance in
the earth. It is one of the 22 minerals essential to the maintenance of the human body.
Calcium, as well as phosphorus and magnesium, are classified as major minerals
because they are found in large amounts in
the body and the daily dietary requirements
exceed 100 mg. In contrast, the trace
minerals such as iron, selenium, and zinc
are present in the body in smaller quantities
and are required in the diet in amounts less
than 20 mg a day. The terms "major" and
"trace" do not reflect the degree of
importance a mineral has in human health
and nutrition; both categories of minerals
are of equal importance.

Calcium is the most plentiful mineral in
the body. Between 1.5% and 2% of an
adult's weight comes from calcium, or
between two to four pounds. Over 99% of

the calcium in the body is found in bones and teeth where it combines in crystals with phosphorus, magnesium, fluoride, zinc, sodium, and other substances to form the rigid skeleton. The skeleton provides support for the soft tissues of the body and holds the body erect. (*Figure 2, Page 22*)

A similar combination of calcium and other minerals is found in the enamel and dentine of teeth. Because the crystals are larger in the teeth than in the bone, the structure is harder and calcium does not move readily in and out of teeth as it does in bone. Even during calcium deficiency, little calcium is lost from the teeth. The remaining 1% of calcium in the body is found in the blood and other fluids of the body where it functions in blood clotting, transmission of nerve impulses, and activation of enzymes and hormones.

The bones serve as a large reservoir of calcium. Throughout the day, calcium is released from bones to be used for nerve transmission or muscle contraction and is absorbed from the blood into the bones when blood levels of the mineral are high, such as after a calcium-rich meal. (*Figure 3, Page 23*)

During the growing years, the balance between calcium deposition and calcium removal from bone is weighted on the side

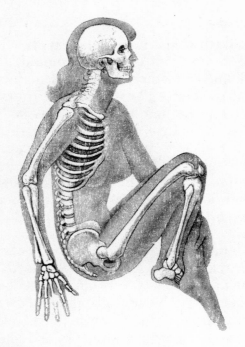

Figure 2.
Over 99% of the calcium in the body is found in the bones and teeth.

of building and more calcium is deposited into bone than is removed. In the healthy adult, the balance between calcium in and calcium out is equal; about 600 mg to 700 mg of calcium enter and leave the bones each day. In later years, especially if the diet

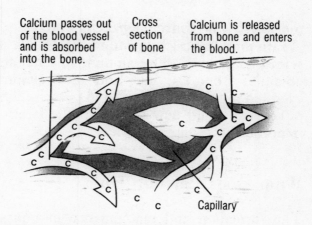

Calcium passes out of the blood vessel and is absorbed into the bone.

Cross section of bone

Calcium is released from bone and enters the blood.

Capillary

Figure 3.   Bone Remodelling
Calcium is released from bones and is absorbed from the blood into the bones.

is low in calcium or a person leads a sedentary life, more calcium is removed from the bone than is deposited.

The blood concentration of calcium must be maintained within a narrow range. The source of this blood calcium is the bones. Hormones, chemical messengers produced in body organs called endocrine glands, are important in maintaining the critical blood level of calcium. When blood levels are low, hormones signal the bones to release calcium into the blood and blood levels increase. When blood levels of calcium are too high, hormones signal the bones to absorb the extra calcium and the blood levels return to normal. The amount of calcium obtained from the diet and the calcium excreted in the urine, stool, and perspiration or used to build new skeletal tissue is also important in calcium balance.

What Does Calcium Do?

The formation and maintenance of bones and teeth are calcium's main functions. The other lesser known functions of calcium are also important.

Blood Clotting

When the body is injured, calcium starts the healing process by stopping the bleeding with the formation of a blood clot. Normal blood calcium levels are maintained constantly to promote this process. Changes in the intake of dietary calcium will not have an effect on blood clotting.

Membranes

Calcium is located in the membranes that surround all body cells. Calcium increases the stability of the membranes and helps regulate the flow of nutrients and other substances into and out of the cell.

Muscle Contraction

Calcium, with the help of magnesium, regulates the contraction and relaxation of muscles. A person can lift a pencil, wash the car, or jog because of the relaxation and contraction of muscles that depend on an adequate amount of calcium. Muscle cramps can be associated with conditions that upset calcium levels in the blood. Calcium is an important contributor to the regulation of the heart beat because the heart is a muscle and the heart beat is a type of muscle contraction. Breathing also is a rhythmic muscle contraction and relaxation and requires calcium for its regulation.

Nerve Transmission

Calcium is essential for transmission of nerve impulses from one nerve to the next. Without adequate calcium in the blood, the nerves become hypersensitive and send improper messages throughout the body. Intermittent and painful spasms of the muscles can result. If blood levels of calcium are too high, nerve transmission is suppressed.

Other Processes

Calcium assists in many important processes in the body. For example, the body's ability to use vitamin B_{12} depends on an adequate concentration of calcium. Many enzymes also are dependent upon calcium. Enzymes work in the body by starting and speeding up chemical reactions. Calcium is essential for the enzymes that convert carbohydrates, proteins, and fats into energy for the body.

Absorption Of Calcium

After a meal, complex digestive processes free the nutrients in the food for use by the body. The process of absorption refers to the transport of nutrients across the lining of the intestine into the blood stream or lymph. Once in the blood stream, nutrients can be used as is or converted to usable substances to perform their vital functions.

Calcium often occurs in combination with other substances in food. Calcium must be separated from these other substances before it is absorbed. This separation is most efficient in an acidic environment. For this reason, most of the absorption of calcium takes place in the upper three-quarters of the small intestine where the concentration of digestive acids is highest.

Humans are inefficient at absorbing calcium from the diet. Healthy adults absorb only 20% to 30% of the calcium ingested. Women who are past menopause absorb as little as 7% of their dietary calcium. There are many factors that also influence calcium absorption. (*Table 1, Page 28*)

Factors That Increase Absorption Of Calcium

Vitamin D: Vitamin D is one of the most important factors in the absorption and use of calcium. Vitamin D regulates calcium movement into and out of bone, and

Table 1	Factors That Influence Calcium Absorption	
	Increased Absorption	**Decreased Absorption**
	Increased need for calcium	Alcohol
		Caffeine
	Lactose (milk sugar)	Some medications
	Vitamin D	High dietary phosphorus
	Zinc (?)	High dietary protein
		Excessive dietary fibre
		Inactivity
		Low vitamin D

improves the body's ability to absorb calcium from the intestine. Vitamin D activates a carrier protein in the intestine that attaches to calcium. Once attached, calcium can cross the intestinal wall into the blood stream. In addition to vitamin D from foods such as vitamin D-fortified milk, exposure to sunlight allows the body to manufacture its own vitamin D. When a person lives in overcast or smoggy areas or is not exposed to adequate amounts of sunlight, the diet becomes an even more important source of this vitamin.

Large doses of vitamin D might have the

opposite effect of moderate intakes and could cause bone to lose its calcium and become weak.

Lactose: Calcium absorption improves when lactose, the sugar found in milk and milk products, is also present. Milk is a good source of both lactose and calcium. Lactose might impair the absorption of calcium in people who do not have sufficient amounts of the enzyme (lactase) to digest lactose. This condition is called lactose intolerance.

High Calcium Need: The body becomes more efficient at absorbing calcium when the need for the mineral is high. Pregnancy, lactation (breastfeeding), and the high rate of growth during childhood and adolescence are conditions that require more calcium. During these stages the body may absorb up to 75% of the available calcium in the diet.

Zinc: Adequate intake of zinc might be necessary for calcium absorption because evidence suggests that zinc influences the transportation of calcium across the intestinal lining into the blood.

Factors That Decrease Absorption Of Calcium

Oxalates And Phytates: Oxalates and phytates are substances found in some foods. They form complexes with calcium in the intestine and hinder absorption of the mineral.

Oxalates are found in rhubarb, kale, spinach, cocoa, and soybeans. These foods also contain significant amounts of calcium. If a person eats a serving of spinach and also drinks a glass of milk, the oxalate might bind the calcium from the spinach but will leave the calcium from the milk free to be used.

Phytates are found in the outer husks of cereals such as oatmeal. People who regularly consume their calcium-rich foods at the same meal with high phytate foods might not benefit from the calcium source as well as if the calcium-rich food were consumed at a separate time from the phytate food. Phytates are destroyed if a whole grain is leavened with yeast and most breads or other grain foods that have added baker's yeast would not reduce calcium absorption.

The Calcium And Phosphorus Balance: Diets that contain about the same amount of calcium and phosphorus (a ratio of 1:1) improve calcium absorption. The average intake of phosphorus is between 800 and 960 mg daily. The ratio of calcium to phosphorus in the diet of most people is 1:2.8, almost three times the recommended ratio. The high phosphorus-low calcium intake might be as the result of a reduced consumption of low-fat dairy foods and increased consumption of meat and phosphorus-containing soft drinks. (*Graph 3, Page 32*)

The calcium:phosphorus ratio has a greater effect on blood levels of calcium than the intake of calcium alone. Excess dietary intake of phosphorus or a poor intake of calcium in relation to phosphorus causes the body to excrete calcium in the urine and increases calcium loss from bones.

Protein Intake: A high-protein diet increases the excretion of calcium in the urine and the dietary requirement for calcium must be increased to compensate for the loss. The average diet is high in protein. People often consume two to three times the advised dietary allowance for protein and this dietary habit, coupled with low calcium and high phosphorus intake, increases the risk of calcium deficiency.

Low Vitamin D Intake: Calcium deficiency and bone disorders can develop in spite of adequate calcium intake if the diet is low in vitamin D. This fat-soluble vitamin is required for calcium to be absorbed and used in the body.

High Fibre Intake: The fibre in whole grain breads and cereals might bind to calcium in the intestine and reduce its absorption. The total fibre intake from a

Graph 3. The Calcium-Phosphorus Ratio Of Selected Foods

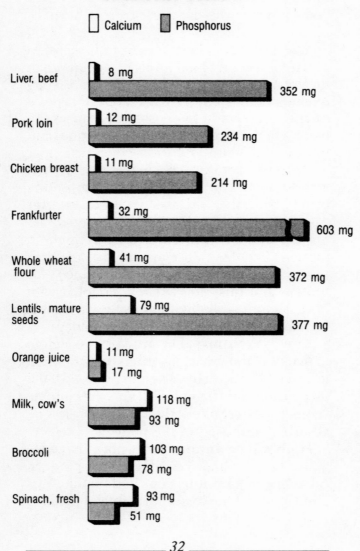

☐ Calcium   ▦ Phosphorus

Liver, beef — 8 mg / 352 mg

Pork loin — 12 mg / 234 mg

Chicken breast — 11 mg / 214 mg

Frankfurter — 32 mg / 603 mg

Whole wheat flour — 41 mg / 372 mg

Lentils, mature seeds — 79 mg / 377 mg

Orange juice — 11 mg / 17 mg

Milk, cow's — 118 mg / 93 mg

Broccoli — 103 mg / 78 mg

Spinach, fresh — 93 mg / 51 mg

diet of whole grain breads and cereals, fresh fruits and vegetables, low-fat dairy products and meats probably will have little effect on calcium absorption. However, if a person consumes large amounts of processed fibre such as bran, and consumes a diet marginal to low in calcium, a calcium deficiency might result.

Alcohol And Drugs: Factors other than diet can also affect the body's use of calcium. While moderate alcohol consumption appears to have no effect, alcoholics absorb calcium less efficiently and might develop abnormal bones. Use of certain drugs such as tetracycline, thyroid preparations, diuretics, and aluminium-containing ant-acids also can decrease absorption of calcium.

Other Lifestyle Factors: Individuals who are bedridden or inactive might absorb less calcium and lose more calcium from the bones. Stress also is associated with an increased loss of calcium and a higher intake of the mineral might be required during stressful times to maintain normal calcium balance.

3

Calcium And Osteoporosis

It is difficult to pick up a newspaper or magazine today without reading about the bone disease osteoporosis. Scientists are trying to determine all the causes of osteoporosis, who is at greatest risk for developing this disease, and what steps might be taken to prevent or cure it.

What Is Osteoporosis?

Osteoporosis is the most common bone disease in the world; one in every four women will develop osteoporosis and around 15 million people currently have it. It is caused by chronic loss of calcium from the bones and is characterised by pain and crippling caused by weak, porous, bones that break easily. Bone loss is a result of ageing and is most commonly seen in advancing years in both men and women. However, the rate of bone loss varies among individuals and with the type of bone affected. Fractures of the hip, wrist and vertebrae (backbone) are common.

Bone Structure

Bone is comprised of a tough framework of protein that is strengthened by deposits of calcium. Mature bone is about 30% protein framework and 70% mineral deposits. The newly formed bones of small children have a higher percentage of framework to mineral content.

The framework of bone is mostly strands of protein fibres, called collagen, that crisscross to form a web. This gives bones the flexibility to withstand pressure without cracking.

The spaces within this protein framework are filled with crystals composed primarily of two minerals, calcium and phosphorus. Other minerals, such as magnesium, fluoride, zinc, and sodium also are found in the framework. These minerals give strength and rigidity to the bone tissue. The more tightly packed the minerals and the larger the crystals that form in bone, the denser and stronger the bone tissue. (*Figure 4, Page 36*)

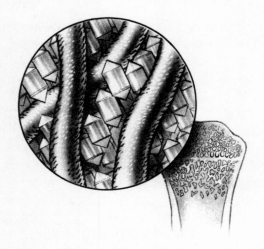

Figure 4.
Mature bone is composed of mineral crystals
embedded in a protein framework.

The protein framework gives bone its
strong tensile strength, or ability to withstand tension. The mineral crystals are quite
like marble and allow bone to resist
compression and withstand the weight of the
body and physical activity. This ability of
bone to withstand pressure and compression
is similar to the qualities of reinforced concrete. The steel rods of reinforced concrete
provide the flexibility and tensile strength
and the cement gives the structure com-

pression strength. Healthy bone, however, is stronger than the finest reinforced concrete.

Bone undergoes continued remodelling throughout life; existing bone minerals are removed and are replaced with new minerals. These processes are known as bone deposition (adding calcium to bone) and bone resorption (removing calcium from bone). Bones reach a maximal strength and density when an individual is 35 years old. After reaching this peak, strength and density continue to decline for the remainder of life, a result of greater bone resorption than deposition.

Bone mass is a measure of the strength or density of the bone. Men have a bone mass 25% to 30% higher than women, so men's bones are more dense. Black people have a 10% higher bone mass than white people, which might explain the reduced incidence of osteoporosis in this population. Reduction of bone mass over time results in weak bones that are more brittle. It is the reduction of bone mass that is a primary cause of the broken bones or fractures seen in osteoporosis.

There are actually two types of bone loss that occur throughout life. The first involves a bone tissue known as cortical or compact bone. This type of bone tissue is found in the long arm and leg bones. Loss of cortical bone escalates after an individual is 50 years old and is often experienced by women after menopause.

The second type of bone loss affects the bones in the spine and pelvis. These bones are called trabecular bones. They are less compact than cortical bone and have a honeycomb-like appearance. As early as the third decade of life both men and women begin to steadily lose trabecular bone.

What Are The Symptoms Of Osteoporosis?

For some individuals the first symptom of osteoporosis is a bone fracture. Other individuals may suffer from years of other aches and pain often attributed to "getting older". Research suggests that bone loss might occur first in the jaw bone, followed by the ribs and vertebrae (bones of the spine). Loss of calcium from the jaw bone, with accompanying pain, could cause further problems by increasing the chances of losing teeth, which would limit the variety of foods and calcium in the diet.

Women suffer from fractures of the spine more often than men. These fractures are known as compression fractures because the vertebrae of the spine are compressed together. Routine activities such as lifting an object or rising from a chair can cause a bone in the spine to collapse if a person has osteoporosis. This type of fracture does not always cause pain and a person may not know it has occurred. It is the repeated collapse of vertebrae that is responsible for the loss of body height (up to 8 inches) and curving of the spine (a widow's hump) that is observed with ageing. (*Figure 5, Page 40*)

Another common fracture seen in osteoporosis is the hip fracture. It is estimated that 190,000 hip fractures occur each year and two-thirds of these are caused by osteoporosis. By age 90, 33% of women and 17% of men have suffered hip fractures. Complications such as hospitalisation, depression, and surgical problems often accompany hip fractures. The complications prove fatal for 12% to 15% of the sufferers, placing hip fractures as the second leading cause of death among people 47 to 74 years old.

The extent of damage from osteoporosis is greater than a loss in height, pain, dental disease, and fractures. Those who survive the hip fracture often lose their mobility and independence and must rely on family, neighbours, or nursing home staff. The

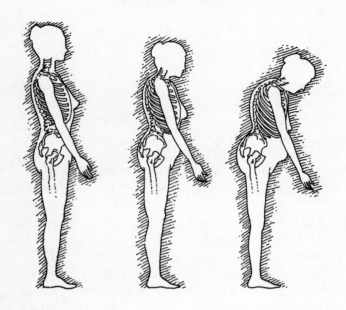

Figure 5.
In osteoporosis, loss of height and curvature of the spine are caused by calcium loss from the bones.

depression or fear of future falls that can accompany the disease reduces the quality of a person's life. The loss of teeth that results from deterioration of the jaw bone can cause eating disorders and malnutrition, which further reduces a person's resistance to disease and infection.

The long-term and serious effects of osteoporosis emphasise the importance of prevention and effective treatment of osteoporosis.

Who Is At Risk Of Developing Osteoporosis?

All people are at risk of developing osteoporosis since bone mass declines with age. However, factors in a person's genetic background and lifestyle can influence the rate of development and extent of damage.

Women: Women are eight times more likely than men to develop osteoporosis. Women's bones are thinner and less dense than men's bones, and less calcium must be lost before the bones are too weak to support the weight of the body. Women tend to live longer than men and because osteoporosis is linked to the ageing process, women are at greater risk of the disease. In addition, women consume less food than men and are more likely to be on weight loss diets that restrict food, and calcium, intake.

White women with a northwestern European ethnic heritage appear to be at greatest risk of developing osteoporosis. These women often have fair complexions with freckles and blond hair. Women of Mediterranean descent have a lower incidence of osteoporosis. Black women seldom suffer from this bone disorder. Osteoporosis is also more common in lean women than in obese women.

Heredity: If a person has inherited a small, thin skeleton, he or she has less calcium to lose before the bones are unable to support the weight of the body. Calcium intake and exercise throughout life are important for these people.

Menopause: Bone mass decreases at a faster rate after menopause. This decline in bone mass after menopause is attributed to a decrease in the blood level of oestrogen, a female hormone produced by the ovaries, and to chronic low intake of calcium throughout life. When oestrogen decreases, bone tissue becomes more sensitive to the hormone, which signals calcium to leave the bone. As a result, the process of bone loss increases after menopause. Women who have an early menopause brought about by surgical removal of the ovaries are at high risk for developing osteoporosis.

It is a mistake to think, however, that osteoporosis begins in later life. Any signs of bone loss at this stage are an indication that the process of calcium depletion has been progressing for years and becomes apparent or is accelerated after menopause.

Low-Calorie Diets: Consumption of a low-calorie diet promotes osteoporosis.

A woman who consumes a low-calorie diet is at risk of developing osteoporosis because a low-calorie diet is often a low-calcium diet. If a woman diets throughout life the likelihood of chronic low intake of calcium increases. A diet of less than 1,600 calories might not supply adequate calcium and supplementation should be considered.

A reliance on regular or diet soft drinks that contain phosphorus can upset the ratio of calcium to phosphorus and increase calcium loss from bones.

Sedentary Lifestyle: Exercise increases bone mass and reduces bone loss. Without physical activity, the bones rapidly lose minerals. The type of exercise most helpful in the prevention of osteoporosis is exercise that puts weight and stress on the long bones of the body. Examples of weightbearing exercise are walking or jogging.

The most dramatic example of the effects of lack of physical activity on bone health can be drawn from the experience of early astronauts. After 72 hours in the weightlessness of space, a group of young astronauts lost significant amounts of calcium from their bones. The effect of weightbearing on bone strength may also explain why slender women are more prone to developing the disorder than their obese counterparts whose skeletons support more pounds.

Stress: The body absorbs less calcium during times of stress, tension, and grief. Stress should be minimised or calcium intake should be increased to compensate for the reduction in absorption.

Pregnancy: At one time it was thought that pregnancy and lactation (breastfeeding) drained calcium from the body and a woman's skeleton would be weakened by her developing baby. More recently it has been observed that women with a history of two or more pregnancies actually have a lower risk of osteoporosis. The preventive effect of pregnancy on osteoporosis might result from the effects of increased weightbearing during the pregnancy.

Medications: Individuals who require long-term use of certain medications also may need calcium supplementation. Corticosteroids can interfere with calcium absorption. The antibiotic tetracycline forms a complex with calcium that interferes with both absorption of calcium and the medication.

Certain types of diuretics (water pills) may cause an increased loss of calcium in the urine. One of the, a drugs used in the treatment of tuberculosis, can depress calcium absorption. Over-the-counter antacids that contain aluminium can also cause problems. (*Table 2, Below*)

The possible interactions of drugs and nutrients can be serious and are often overlooked. Individuals who take the medications listed below should consult their doctors before adding any supplements or over-the-counter medications to their health care programme.

Table 2	Medications That May Affect Calcium
1.	Corticosteroids (anti-inflammatory)
2.	Anticonvulsants
3.	Drugs for Paget's disease
4.	Diuretics
5.	Sedatives
6.	Drugs for Tuberculosis

Coffee Drinkers: Caffeine increases the amount of calcium excreted in the urine. High intakes of caffeine beverages (6 or more cups of coffee daily) might lead to a negative calcium balance where more calcium is lost from the system than is replaced. While the best plan is to be moderate in caffeine consumption, those unwilling to lower their intake might need to consider use of a calcium supplement.

Cigarettes And Alcohol: Cigarette smoking and a heavy intake of alcohol are other habits associated with the development of osteoporosis.

Diagnosis Of Osteoporosis

The lack of simple, objective tests to measure bone loss has made the study of osteoporosis difficult. There is no blood or urine test that can diagnose osteoporosis. There are several methods available to measure bone density. These techniques vary in their cost, availability, and, since they rely on X-rays, radiation dosage. In addition, as much as 30% of bone must be lost before a standard X-ray will detect the presence of osteoporosis.

Bone depletion can first be detected in the bone of the jaw, called the alveolar bone. This depletion of bone tissue occurs much earlier than osteoporosis and is associated with a reduced intake of calcium. If bone loss is detected at this point, the process might be reversed by increasing the consumption of calcium to at least a level of 800 mg daily.

A method of detecting the early stages of osteoporosis is called Radiographic Densitometry. It uses common dental surgery X-ray equipment and allows evaluation of bone status during a person's routine dental examination.

Prevention of Osteoporosis

The pain and suffering caused by osteoporosis might be prevented. While treatment of osteoporosis is possible, the best defence is prevention.

Prevention begins early. If a person is between 20 and 40 years old, he or she has reached adult height. Bones have reached maximum length and width and unless careful attention is paid to diet and exercise, bones will begin to lose calcium.

If a person is more than 40 years old, the bones have begun their thinning process. Although this is a normal process, if it proceeds too quickly or lasts for a long time, the possibility of osteoporosis increases. The rate of bone loss can be slowed if calcium intake is increased and "weight-bearing" exercise is a part of the daily routine.

The following steps will help prevent this disease:

1. Consume adequate calcium (500 mg to 1,200 mg) and vitamin D (400 IU) throughout adult life. After menopause, women who are not receiving oestrogen therapy should consume about 1,500 mg of calcium per day.
2. Engage in weightbearing exercise such as walking or jogging on a daily basis.
3. Avoid cigarette smoking. Women who smoke reach menopause several years earlier than non-smokers and are at increased risk of developing osteoporosis.
4. Do not take large doses of vitamins A and D. Excesses of these vitamins will cause the body to lose strengthening minerals from the bones. (*Figure 6, Opposite*)

Treatment Of Osteoporosis

Treatment of osteoporosis is similar to the recommendations for prevention. Early detection is essential to begin treatment of osteoporosis before a disabling fracture occurs.

Oestrogen Replacement: Oestrogen levels decline at menopause. For women

Figure 6.   Foods High In Calcium

1. **Milk Group**
   Nonfat milk
   Yogurt, plain
   Swiss cheese

2. **Fruit-Vegetable Group**
   Spinach
   Turnip greens

3. **Grain Group**
   Corn based products

4. **Dried Beans And Meat Group**
   Beans, dried,
      cooked
   Salmon, with bones
   Sardines, with bones
   Tofu, processed
      with calcium sulfate

entering menopause, one of the most effective forms of treatment for osteoporosis might be oestrogen replacement therapy. Women who receive oestrogen replacement therapy within a few years of menopause have fewer hip and wrist fractures than those who do not receive treatment.

Oestrogen replacement therapy, however, might increase the risk of some types of cancer such as cancers of the uterine lining. Oestrogen replacement therapy might not be appropriate for all women.

Calcium And Vitamin D Supplements: Supplements that combine both calcium and vitamin D are another common treatment for osteoporosis. Individuals need more vitamin D as they get older. People in northern climates or older people who are not exposed to enough sunlight may have difficulty meeting their vitamin D requirement. In addition, older adults might not produce as much vitmain D in the skin, even when they are in the sun, as they did in former years. As a result, adding a moderate amount of vitamin D to a calcium supplement might make the treatment more effective. To avoid possible toxic effects, no one should consume more than 600 to 800 IU of vitamin D daily.

Fluoride: People who grow to adulthood in areas with a high fluoride level in the water have a lower incidence of osteoporosis than those who are in a low fluoride area. Fluoride is effective in increasing the bone mass in the spine and hip. One major side effect of fluoride is gastrointestinal irritation. It is still too soon to say whom fluoride might help and how to determine the ideal dosage.

Can Osteoporosis Be Reversed?

There is evidence that some of the bone loss of osteoporosis might be reversed if discovered early and promptly treated.

One study used calcium and vitamin D supplementation in a group of elderly women aged 79 to 89 years old. After three years of consuming an intake of over 1,000 mg calcium per day, these women had a bone density 12% higher than similar women who consumed an average of 450 mg of calcium per day.

In another experiment, healthy women 37 to 73 years old were given 750 mg of calcium combined with 375 IU of vitamin D. After 36 months on this regimen, the women showed an average increase in bone density of 12.5%.

The density of the jaw bones in a group of people was increased by giving each of them 1,000 mg of calcium daily for 12 months. Jaw bone strength and tooth disorders are improved when calcium intake is increased.

Exercise also has been used to increase bone density. In a group of 73 postmeno-pausal women, those who participated in exercises of walking or dancing increased their bone strength. A similar group of women who did not exercise continued to lose bone mass. Results of these studies offer hope for those who are already experiencing some of the debilitating symptoms of osteoporosis.

People who want to reduce their risk of

osteoporosis should consume a diet adequate in calcium and vitamin D, avoid cigarette smoking and use of excessive vitamin D or vitamin A supplements, and engage in regular weightbearing exercise. Currently treatment for osteoporosis relies on oestrogen replacement therapy and supplementation with calcium and vitamin D.

4

Calcium And Hypertension

Blood pressure is the pumping force of the heart as it sends blood through the arteries to all tissues of the body. Each time the heart beats, the blood pressure increases momentarily. This is called systolic blood pressure. Between beats, the heart relaxes as it refills with blood. The residual pressure in the arteries between beats is called diastolic blood pressure.

Blood pressure is measured by placing a rubber cuff around the upper arm and inflating the cuff with air. This inflated cuff presses against the artery and closes it off. As the air is released gradually from the cuff, the blood begins to flow again through the artery and the presure at which it flows is recorded on a measuring gauge or digital read-out.

Many people suffer from high blood pressure (hypertension). Hypertension is excessive pressure of the blood against the walls of the heart and arteries. Hypertension is diagnosed when a person has a blood pressure reading that averages 160/95 or more on two or more successive occasions. Blood pressure varies during the day and from one day to another. Hypertension occurs when the blood pressure remains elevated.

Blood Pressure Values

	Systolic/Diastolic
Normal	120/80 or less
Borderline	140/90 to 160/95
Hypertension	160/95 or more

Blood pressure is regulated by a thin layer of muscle that surrounds the artery walls. The muscle can expand (relax) to increase the diameter of the artery and allow more blood to move through with less pressure when blood pressure is too high. The muscle can constrict (contract) to reduce the diameter of the artery and increase blood pressure when the pressure falls too low.

Hypertension occurs when muscles of the arteries contract and stay contracted, when blood volume increases, or when the heart's pumping action increases. Regardless of the origin, hypertension is a result of either an

Graph 4.
Hypertension occurs when muscles of the arteries contract, when blood volume increases, or when the heart's pumping action increases.

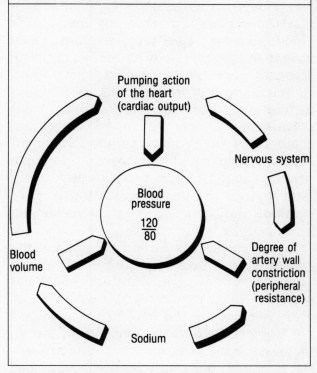

increased blood volume or reduced diameter of the arteries. (*Graph 4, Above*)

For 90% of people with high blood pressure there is no known cause. This type of hypertension is called "essential hypertension". The remaining 10% have hypertension that can be attributed to another disease such as a tumour on the adrenal gland or diabetes. This type of hypertension is called "secondary hypertension".

Many factors influence an individual's blood pressure: age, race, heredity, body weight and percent body fat, stress, cigarette smoking, oral contraceptives, pregnancy, exercise, and nutrition. Certain medications including oral contraceptives, steroids, nasal decongestants, appetite suppressants, and some types of antidepressants also might cause secondary hypertension in some people. Blood pressure tends to increase in individuals with age. Hypertension is more common and occurs at an earlier age among black people.

Hypertension has earned the label of the "silent killer" because those who have it often do not have symptoms and might not seek the necessary medical care. Two in every five people who have hypertension do not know they have it. Feelings of stress, increased heart beat, or being "uptight" are not symptoms of hypertension. The only way to detect hypertension is to have regular blood pressure checks.

Hypertension is dangerous because it accelerates the process of atherosclerosis and heart disease. People with hypertension have a two to three times greater chance of developing heart disease, and a three times greater chance of having a stroke than people with normal blood pressure. People with hypertension have an increased risk of developing blood clots that can block an already cholesterol-clogged artery and cut off blood supply to the heart or brain. Elevated blood pressure weakens the arteries and encourages them to break (aneurism). Although hypertension (high blood pressure) is a major risk factor for developing cardiovascular disease (CVD), congestive heart failure, stroke, and chronic kidney failure, the risks of disability or death from hypertension can be reduced with proper treatment. (*Figure 7, Page 58*)

Nutrition And Hypertension

Nutrition is important in the cause, prevention, and treatment of hypertension. In the past, studies relating nutrition and hypertension focused on sodium. Sodium is a mineral found in table salt. Sodium also is used as a food additive, such as monosodium glutamate (MSG) and the sodium nitrite in processed meats.

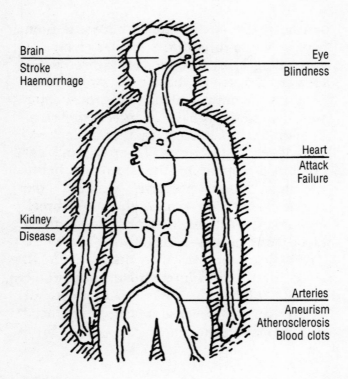

Figure 7.
Hypertension is a risk factor
for developing cardiovascular disease,
congestive heart failure, stroke, eye
disorders, and kidney disease.

Studies that compare large population
groups throughout the world show that the
higher the salt intake of the people in a
country, the higher the blood pressure of its

people. In areas of South Africa and New Guinea where sodium intake is very low (200 to 1,400 mg daily), hypertension is almost absent. High blood pressure is prevalent in northern Japan, where the intake of sodium often exceeds 9,200 mg per day.

Not everyone who consumes a high-salt diet develops hypertension, which implies that some people might be salt-sensitive.

In recent years, researchers have begun to look at other nutrients for their possible role in hypertension. Studies have shown that dietary calcium has an effect on blood pressure.

Calcium And Hypertension

The link between calcium intake and risk of hypertension is not new. Observations in the early 1900s showed people who lived in areas with hard water had less heart disease. Hard water contains calcium while soft water has a low calcium and high sodium content. This finding led researchers to study calcium and its effect on blood pressure. Nutritional studies have linked calcium intake to blood pressure levels.

The results of these nutrition surveys are interesting. Although the dietary intake of calcium in people with hypertension is lower than in healthy people, the intake is within the "normal" range. If people with hypertension require an increased intake of calcium to prevent or treat hypertension, the advised dietary allowance might not be sufficient for these people.

Supporting the belief that a low calcium intake also might be associated with hypertension is a study that found two to three times more hypertension among women with osteoporosis than women without this bone disorder.

Not only is a deficiency of calcium linked to hypertension, but when calcium intake is increased blood pressure often decreases. This effect on blood pressure is seen in healthy people, and people with mild to severe hypertension. The earlier calcium supplementation is started, the greater the long-term effects on lowering blood pressure.

Just how a higher calcium intake might protect against hypertension is not well understood. One theory links calcium in the maintenance of the muscles that surround arteries and help regulate blood pressure.

Another theory states that calcium and magnesium balance at the cellular level might have an effect on blood pressure. Normally, calcium concentration is low within the cell and high outside the cell. Magnesium concentration is the reverse, high within the cell and low outside the cell. This difference in concentrations is maintained by a pumping mechanism in the cell membrane. If the pumping action is defective, these differences in calcium and magnesium concentrations might not be maintained. Too much magnesium might leak out of the cell or too much calcium might leak into the cell. This might disturb the hormone that regulates blood pressure and lead to hypertension. If this theory is correct, some people would respond to magnesium supplementation and others would respond to calcium supplementation.

There might be a link between sodium and calcium intake and hypertension. A diet high in sodium is associated with hypertension and with an increased excretion of calcium. Whether sodium's link with hypertension is independent of calcium or is secondary to an effect of calcium loss has not been determined.

Although the evidence is supportive, the link between calcium and hypertension is not proven. Low blood levels of calcium might be a result of hypertension rather than the cause, in which case an increase in dietary calcium would not benefit the person with elevated blood pressure.

However, if low intake of calcium is a cause of hypertension, increased dietary intake or supplementation would be beneficial.

Calcium intake has declined and is below acceptable levels in some segments of the population, particularly the older adults; populations that are at high risk for hypertension.

It is too early to make a specific recommendation regarding the amount of calcium a hypertensive person should consume; however, the consumption of a diet that is adequate in calcium, at least 800 mg, would be a beginning. As research progresses, calcium supplementation may emerge as a valuable, inexpensive means of treatment for some people with hypertension. (*Table 3, Below*)

Table 3 Calcium Equivalents
The following foods provide the same amount of calcium as an 8 ounce glass of nonfat milk:
250 ml/8 fl oz/1 cup calcium-fortified soy milk
175 g/6 oz/1 cup broccoli
175 g/6 oz/1 cup almonds
175 g/6 oz/1½ cups kale
225 g/8 oz/1⅔ cups sunflower seeds
225 g/8 oz/2 cups quick-cooking, enriched flour
450 g/1 lb/3 cups cooked dried beans

Other Nutritional Factors And Hypertension

Calories: Calorie intake might be the most important dietary factor in the development of hypertension. An increase in weight is associated with an increase in blood pressure. Obese individuals have higher blood pressure levels than people who are at their ideal body weight. Weight reduction lowers blood pressure even when sodium intake remains constant.

Fat: Some polyunsaturated fats might lower blood pressure by their effect on relaxing the muscles in the artery wall. However, a diet high in fat, especially saturated fats from dairy and animal products, might increase blood pressure.

Magnesium: Magnesium is another mineral that might be important in the regulation of blood pressure. Evidence suggests that magnesium may offer as much protection as calcium against hypertension.

Potassium And Sodium Balance: Potassium and sodium interact together in the body, and the balance of these two minerals might be a factor in blood pressure. High-sodium processed foods, such as potato crisps, often replace high-potassium foods, such as fresh fruits and vegetables.

This high sodium-low potassium diet might be a factor in hypertension. In some cases, an increase in dietary potassium lowers blood pressure. (*Table 4, Opposite*)

Chloride: Table salt is composed of the two elements sodium and chloride. Although sodium is the primary component of salt associated with hypertension, some evidence suggests that chloride also might be involved. Some animals develop hypertension when fed sodium chloride (table salt) but maintain normal blood pressure when fed nonchloride-containing sodium.

Other Trace Nutrients: Several trace minerals and vitamins might be involved in the regulation of blood pressure. The trace minerals, including chromium, cobalt, copper, manganese, molybdenum, selenium, vanadium, and zinc, are involved in processes important to cardiovascular health. Several vitamins including vitamin E, vitamin A, vitamin C, and the B vitamins are necessary for the maintenance of cell membranes and other body structures that help regulate blood pressure.

Summary: Hypertension is a serious disorder that affects a large portion of the population. In most cases, the exact cause of hypertension is not known. Various nutritional factors have been implicated in the cause of hypertension. Manipulating the

Table 4	The Highs And Lows Of Sodium

Emphasise These Foods Low In Sodium
  Unsalted seasonings
  Unsalted grain products
  Baked products made without salt, baking
    powder or baking soda
  Fruits
  Fruit juices
  Unsalted vegetables
  Fresh meat prepared without salt
  Dried beans cooked without salt or salt pork
  Unsalted nuts
  Ricotta cheese
  Most mineral waters (check with supplier)

Use In Moderation Foods Medium In Sodium
  Lightly salted seasonings
  Tomato puree or sauce
  Grain products made with small amounts of
    salt, baking powder, or baking soda
  Biscuits
  Lightly salted vegetables
  Tinned vegetables
  Fresh shellfish
  Milk
  Yogurt

Beware Of These Foods High In Sodium
  Salt
  Highly salted seasonings
  Highly salted grain products
  Pretzels
  Salted crackers and crisps
  Salted popcorn
  Highly salted vegetables
  All pickled vegetables
  Olives and pickles
  Sauerkraut
  Smoked, cured or pickled products
  Bacon
  Luncheon meats
  Processed cheese products

Figure 8.   The Antihypertension Diet

diet, especially to reduce its sodium content, is a popular treatment for hypertension. Calcium has recently emerged as an important nutrient that might prevent hypertension. (*Figure 8, Above*)

Many questions remain unanswered about calcium and hypertension. As research progresses these questions should be answered. Meanwhile, the safest course of action is for all individuals with hypertension, and those at risk of this disorder, to consume diets that contain at least the recommended daily amount of calcium.

5

Calcium And Other Health Problems

Calcium might be involved in the treatment and prevention of other diseases and conditions in addition to osteoporosis and hypertension.

Alzheimer's Disease

An excessive accumulation of aluminium has been observed in the brains of patients with Alzheimer's Disease. Adequate intake of calcium might reduce the toxic effects and accumulation of aluminium in tissues.

Vitamin D And Bowel Cancer

Calcium and vitamin D might offer some protection against cancer of the colon and rectum. In examining a group of 1,527 men, those of them who developed bowel cancer consumed less calcium and vitamin D than those who remained free of disease. Insufficient evidence exists, however, to recommend an increase in calcium beyond the current advised dietary allowance to prevent or treat bowel cancer.

Cardiovascular Disease

Calcium might reduce blood cholesterol levels in some individuals. Elevated blood cholesterol is a risk factor for cardiovascular disease (CVD) and a reduction in blood cholesterol is associated with a reduced risk for CVD. People who have high cholesterol levels sometimes show a reduction in these levels if calcium supplements of 1,000 mg per day are included in the diet.

Eclampsia Of Pregnancy

Eclampsia is a serious complication of pregnancy that is fatal to the foetus in 30% to 35% of the cases. The disorder is characterised by hypertension, oedema (bloating and swelling of the legs or ankles), and protein loss in the urine. Eclampsia, also called toxaemia of pregnancy or pre-eclampsia, usually develops in the last three months of pregnancy. The cause of eclampsia is not known but several factors including poor prenatal care, poor nutrition, and first pregnancy are associated with the disease. Low intake of calcium might be related to the development of eclampsia.

A nutritious diet combined with a vitamin-mineral supplement that contains calcium might reduce the incidence of eclampsia.

Kidney Stones

About 1 in 1,000 adults develops urinary tract stones and is hospitalised as a result of complications. Kidney stones are composed of crystals of calcium combined with other substances such as oxalate or phosphate. The formation of crystals depends upon the concentration of these substances in the urine; when the concentration is high, stones are more likely to form. Those people who form stones excrete large quantities of calcium, thus increasing the concentration of calcium in the urine. Calcium supplements are not recommended for those people prone to developing kidney stones. A doctor should be consulted by those people at risk of developing kidney stones, and a diet should be designed that supplies them with the proper amount of dietary calcium to prevent both osteoporosis and kidney stone formation.

Periodontal Disease

Diseases of the gums are called periodontal diseases. They are a major cause of tooth loss in adults. Evidence shows that calcium supplementation of 1,000 to 2,000 mg a day over several months might reduce the incidence of periodontal disorders. A diet low in calcium might contribute to the progression of this disease. Inadequate dietary calcium is linked to loss of calcium from the jaw bone (alveolar bone), which makes dentures difficult to position. Daily brushing and flossing also are important in the prevention of dental disease.

6
Calcium Supplements

Who Might Benefit From Calcium Supplementation?

Many people do not consume sufficient calcium, and calcium supplements are one way to meet daily requirements.

Women might benefit most from regular calcium supplementation because they consume less calcium and food than men consume. Women also are at higher risk of developing osteoporosis. However, careful consideration of calcium intake is important for all ages, male and female, since anyone can develop osteoporosis.

There are subgroups of people who are at higher risk than others of developing osteoporosis.

- Postmenopausal women,
- People who diet,
- People who are small-boned,

- People who consume several cups of coffee each day,
- People who take medications that reduce calcium absorption, such as tetracycline and aluminium-containing antacids,
- People who smoke cigarettes,
- Women who have had their ovaries surgically removed, and
- People under chronic stress.

Are All Calcium Supplements Similar?

All calcium supplements are not the same. Calcium is combined with other compounds in supplements. There are five primary types of calcium preparations available. These are:

- Calcium gluconate
- Calcium lactate
- Calcium phosphate
- Calcium carbonate
- Calcium citrate

In healthy individuals, all calcium supplements are absorbed in the same way and are considered good sources of the mineral. However, some disorders might affect the absorption of different calcium preparations. Calcium requires an acidic environment in the intestine to be absorbed. People with achlorhydria (poor secretion of stomach acid) might not efficiently absorb calcium carbonate. A supplement of calcium citrate, or consuming calcium carbonate with a meal, might improve the absorption of calcium.

Another difference between calcium supplements is the amount of calcium they contain. Calcium carbonate has the most calcium; it is 40% calcium, 60% carbonate. Calcium phosphate contains 29% calcium. Calcium lactate and calcium gluconate both contain between 9% and 13% calcium. People who take calcium must consider this percentage factor when determining how much calcium they are ingesting. (*Table 5, Page 74*)

Some antacid preparations contain large amounts of calcium carbonate and are an excellent source of calcium. One advantage of this type of product is that the tablets are chewable and often come in a variety of flavours. Use of antacids appears to be a safe practice providing the product does not contain aluminium. Aluminium reduces calcium absorption and encourages the development of bone disorders.

Supplements of bone meal and dolomite might be contaminated with trace amounts of some toxic metals such as lead, arsenic,

Table 5 The Amount Of Calcium In Different Supplements			
Calcium Salt	Theoretical Tablet Size	Percent Calcium	Content Of Elemental Calcium
Calcium gluconate	1200 mg	9	108 mg
Calcium lactate	1200 mg	13	156 mg
Calcium phosphate	1200 mg	29	348 mg
Calcium carbonate	1200 mg	40	480 mg

mercury, and cadmium. These sources of calcium should be avoided unless it can be verified that there is no contamination.

Vitamin D is an important regulator of calcium absorption by the body. Before vitamin D can perform its functions in the body, the liver must convert it into an active form. It is this active form that is needed for the absorption of calcium and the regulation of calcium into and out of bone. Older adults might be less efficient at manufacturing vitamin D in the presence of sunlight and at converting vitamin D to its active form. Older adults might also receive less exposure to sunlight and consume fewer foods fortified with vitamin

D, making them at higher risk for marginal deficiencies of this nutrient.

Several supplements of calcium contain vitamin D to help boost the body's absorption of calcium. Daily intake of vitamin D should not exceed 800 IU or a level twice the advised dietary allowance because vitamin D can be toxic at large doses. If selecting a supplement with both calcium and vitamin D, the dosage of each nutrient must be considered.

For people who choose to take calcium supplements or are instructed to do so by their doctors, the amount needed may depend on several factors:

- The amount of calcium consumed in foods. A milk drinker can get approximately 300 mg of calcium in an 8 oz glass. Two glasses of milk a day would usually meet the advised dietary allowance while those requiring more may benefit from a supplement. An individual who is lactose intolerant, dieting, or who dislikes milk might consume far less than 800 mg per day and require more calcium by supplementation.

- Age, gender, physical activity level, and identified risk factors for developing osteoporosis. Premenopausal women or women treated with oestrogen should consume 1,000 mg of calcium daily. Post-menopausal women who do not receive oestrogen treatment should consume 1,500 mg of calcium daily. Achieving these intake levels through diet alone might be difficult.

- Medical conditions or treatments that affect the need for nutrient supplementation. Some conditions may require more calcium and supplements are needed to meet the higher requirements. For others, calcium supplements could be hazardous. A pharmacist should be consulted regarding medication-calcium interactions.

Are Large Doses Of Calcium Harmful?

Calcium intakes in the range of 1,000 to 2,500 mg daily do not cause problems for normal, healthy individuals.

Information on the effects of large doses of calcium (10,000 mg a day) is limited. If the mineral is hazardous in large amounts it might be because of its effect on the body's balance of other nutrients. Excess intake of calcium might inhibit the absorption of zinc and cause a zinc deficiency. The effect of large doses of calcium on zinc cannot be counteracted with an increased intake of zinc, since large doses of zinc might cause an iron or copper deficiency. Iron absorption and tissue stores might decline when calcium intake is too high.

Large doses of calcium in animals sometimes results in a secondary deficiency of vitamin K and excessive bleeding. Finally, a large intake of calcium might upset the ratio of calcium to phosphorus and result in bone loss.

Calcium supplements can cause minor problems for healthy people. Some people experience constipation, bloating, or intestinal gas. These problems are not serious but can be annoying. Calcium supplements can reduce the effectiveness of tetracycline and should be taken at a different time of the day than the medication.

Calcium supplementation might not be beneficial for people with certain disorders. People with a history of kidney problems should avoid calcium supplementation unless it is specifically prescribed by a doctor.

Persons who suffer from peptic ulcer disease may be susceptible to problems from excess calcium intake. A syndrome described as the "milk-alkalai syndrome" occurs in individuals who consume large amounts of milk along with quantities of antacids. These individuals develop abnormally high levels of calcium in their blood and are more likely to develop kidney problems.

Summary

The aches and pains, stooped posture, loss of teeth, and bone fractures of osteoporosis and an elevation in blood pressure were once called the inevitable result of "old age". It is now recognised that these diseases are influenced by a lifetime of habits.

The choices a person makes about diet, exercise, and other health habits will have an effect on whether the bones remain strong and upright or become porous and hunched, and whether the blood pressure and heart will remain healthy.

Worksheet 1 What Is Your Calcium Intake?

Food	Portion of	No. of servings	Calcium Mg	Total Calcium
Plain Low-fat Yogurt	250ml/8fl oz/1 cup			
Non-fat Dry Milk Powder	50g/2oz/½ cup			
Tinned Sardines	small tin		× 400 =	
	Total servings			
Fruit Flavoured Yogurt	250ml/8fl oz/1 cup			
Skimmed and Low-fat Milk	250ml/8fl oz/1 cup			
Whole Milk, Choc. Milk	250ml/8fl oz/1 cup			
Parmesan Cheese (grated)	25g/1oz/¼ cup			
Swiss and Gruyere Cheese	25g/1oz/3 tbsp			
	Total servings		× 300 =	
Cheese (all other hard cheese)	25g/1oz/3 tbsp			
Enriched flour (instant, cooked)	100g/4oz/1 cup			
	Total servings		× 200 =	
Tinned Pink Salmon	small tin			
Tofu (processed with calcium)	100g/4oz/½ cup			
	Total servings		× 150 =	

Food	Serving	Total servings		
Ice Cream	100g/4oz/½ cup			
Spinach, cooked	100g/4oz/½ cup			
Broccoli, cooked	75g/3oz/½ cup			
	Total servings	____ × 75 =		
Almonds	25g/1oz/3 tbsp			
Soybeans, cooked	75g/3oz/½ cup			
Cottage Cheese	100g/4oz/½ cup			
Orange	1 med			
Kidney Beans, Cooked	75g/3oz/½ cup			
	Total servings	____ × 50 =		
Carrot, raw	1 med			
Dates & raisins	40g/1½oz/¼ cup			
Egg	1 large			
Whole Wheat Bread	1 slice			
Peanut Butter	2 tbsp			
	Total servings	____ × 25 =		

My Actual Calcium Intake

Less My Advised Dietary Allowance For Calcium

The Difference is

Glossary

Alveolar Bone: The jaw bone.

Artery: Blood vessel that carries blood and oxygen from the heart to the tissues.

Bacteria: Microscopic one-celled organisms found in food and in the body.

Caffeine: A drug that stimulates the nervous system and is found in coffee, tea, and some soft drinks.

Calorie: A measurement of heat. In nutrition, calorie refers to the quantity of energy contained in foods.

Cardiovascular Disease: A disease of the heart and blood vessels often caused by an accumulation of cholesterol in the lining of the blood vessels.

Cholesterol: A type of fat found in foods from animal sources and also produced by the liver. High levels of cholesterol in the blood are associated with the development of cardiovascular disease.

Collagen: A protein found in connective tissue, bone, skin, and tendons that holds cells and other substances together.

Cortical Bone: A type of bone found in the long bones of the arms and legs, characterised by a dense, compacted appearance.

Dowager's Hump: The hunched appearance common in people with osteoporosis. The chest also might be collapsed and the abdomen protruded.

Eclampsia: A disorder that occurs in the latter three months of pregnancy, characterised by fluid retention, hypertension, protein loss in the urine, convulsions, or coma.

Enzyme: Protein-like substances in the body that initiate and accelerate chemical reactions.

Hormone: A chemical substance produced by the endocrine glands that is released into the blood and transported to another organ or tissue, where it performs a specific action. Examples of hormones are oestrogen, adrenalin, and insulin.

Hypertension: High blood pressure.

Lactation: Breastfeeding.

Lactose: Milk sugar.

Lactose Intolerance: Inability to digest milk sugar (lactose) because of a deficit of lactase, the enzyme that digests lactose.

Metabolism: The total of all body processes that converts foods into tissues, breaks down and repairs tissues, and converts complex substances into simple ones for energy.

Obesity: body weight more than 20% above desirable weight; excessive body fat.

Oestrogen: The female sex hormone that aids in the regulation of ovulation and sex characteristics.

Osteoporosis: Loss of calcium from the bones that results in porous, weak bones that are prone to fractures.

Oxalate: A substance in foods, such as spinach, that binds with calcium and reduces the absorption of the mineral.

Periodontal Disease: Diseases of the tissues that surround the teeth.

Polyunsaturated Fat: The type of fat found in vegetable oils, nuts, and seeds, and in smaller amounts in fish and chicken.

Phytate: A compound found in unleavened whole grain cereals that binds to calcium in the intestine and reduces its absorption.

Resorption: Removal of calcium from bone by dissolving into the blood.

Sodium: A mineral found in table salt and foods, which is linked to hypertension.

Trabecular bone: A type of bone that is found in the spine and pelvis, characterised by a honeycomb appearance.

Vertebrae: Any one of the 33 bones in the spinal column.

Vitamins Checklist –
Needs and Sources

Vitamin A
Daily requirement
    adults   up to 1mg
    children   0.4mg rising to 1mg
Sources
    4oz./110g ox liver   6.8mg
    4oz./110g cooked carrots   2.25mg
    1 halibut liver oil capsule   1.2mg
    4oz./110g cooked
      spinach   1.15mg

Vitamin B1 (thiamin)
Daily requirement
    adults   1.25mg
    children   0.5mg rising to 1mg
Sources
    1oz./25g cereal +
      4fl.oz./½ cup semi-
      skim milk   0.4mg
    1 large slice of bread   0.15mg
    4oz./110g potato   0.1mg

Vitamin B2 (riboflavin)
Daily requirement
    adults   1.5mg
    children   0.8mg rising to 1.5mg
Sources
    4oz./110g liver   3.5mg

6oz./160g cabbage or Brussels sprouts	1.5mg
1oz./25g cereal + 4fl.oz./½ cup semi-skim milk	0.6mg
1 egg	0.25mg

Vitamin B6 (pyridoxine)
Daily requirement
adults	2mg
children	1.5mg rising to 2mg

Sources
1 banana	480mg
1 orange	90mg
1 egg	50mg

NB Remember that Vitamin B6 is destroyed by heat, light and air.

Vitamin B12
Daily requirement
adults and children	3 micrograms

Sources
6oz./160g meat	2 micrograms
1oz./25g cereal + 4fl.oz./½ cup semi-skim milk	1 microgram
8fl.oz./1 cup milk	1 microgram

Folic Acid
Daily requirement
adults and children	400 micrograms

Sources
1 tablespoon brewers yeast	313 micrograms
4oz./110g cooked spinach	165 micrograms
6fl.oz. orange juice	102 micrograms
1oz./25g cereal + 4fl.oz./½ cup semi-skim milk	80 micrograms

NB Remember that pregnant women, nursing mothers and women taking an oral contraceptive need extra folic acid.

Niacin
Daily requirement

men	18mg
women	13mg
children	6mg rising to 18mg

Sources

6oz./160g beef	12mg
1oz./25g cereal + 4fl.oz./ ½ cup semi-skim milk	4.6mg
1oz./25g cheese	1.75mg
1 egg	1.65mg

Vitamin C
Daily requirement

adults	30mg–60mg
children	15mg–30mg

Sources

4oz./110g fresh blackcurrants	220mg
1 orange	60mg
4oz./110g Brussels sprouts	40mg

Vitamin D
Daily requirement

adults	10 micrograms
children	7.5 micrograms

Sources

cod liver oil capsule (check dose)	up to 10 micrograms
1oz./25g cereal + 4fl.oz./ ½ cup semi-skim milk	0.6 micrograms

NB Remember that much of the vitamin D requirement is satisfied by exposure to normal amounts of sunlight.

Energy and Minerals Checklist – Needs and Sources

Protein

Daily requirement

men	56 grams
women	44 grams

Sources

6oz./160g turkey	55 grams
8fl.oz./1 cup low fat milk	8 grams
1oz./25g cereal + 4fl.oz./ ½ cup semi-skim milk	6 grams
1 slice wholewheat bread	2.5 grams

Calories

Daily requirement

men	2,000 kcal
women	1,500 kcal

NB People taking strenuous physical exercise add up to 1,000 kcal

Sources

6oz./160g grilled steak	350 kcal
6oz./160g roast chicken without skin	240 kcal
6oz./160g cod or haddock	120 kcal
6oz./160g chips	420 kcal
medium baked potato	150 kcal
1oz./25g slice of bread	70 kcal
1oz./25g butter	225 kcal

1oz./25g cheddar cheese	115 kcal
½ pint/10fl.oz. semi-skim milk	125 kcal
1 chocolate digestive biscuit	85 kcal
½ pint/10fl.oz. beer (bitter)	100 kcal
5fl.oz. dry white wine	95 kcal

Fibre

Daily requirement adults and children	30 grams
Sources	
1 orange	5.4 grams
1 medium baked potato	5.2 grams
1 slice wholewheat bread	2.7 grams
2 slices wholewheat crispbread	2.6 grams
1oz./25g bran flakes + 4fl.oz./ ½ cup semi-skim milk	2.5 grams

Calcium

Daily requirement	
adults	500mg
teenagers and pregnant women	1,200mg
Sources	
3oz./80g boiled spinach	500mg
8fl.oz./1 cup milk	300mg
1oz./25g cheese	250mg
1oz./25g cereal + 4fl.oz./ ½ cup semi-skim milk	160mg
1 tablespoon non-fat dried milk	52mg

Copper

Daily requirement adults and children	2mg

Sources
    6oz./160g ox liver   4.75mg
    8fl.oz./1 cup whole milk   0.09mg

Iron
Daily requirement
    adults and children   12mg
Sources
    1oz./25g cereal + 4fl.oz./
      1 cup semi-skim milk   2.1mg

Potassium
Daily requirement
    adults and children   2–3 grams
Sources
    1oz./25g cornflakes + 4fl.oz./
      1 cup semi-skim milk   200mg
    1oz./25g oatmeal   111mg
    8fl.oz./1 cup whole milk   340mg

Sodium
Daily requirement
    adults and children   1–3 grams
Sources
    1 teaspoon salt   2.3 grams
    1oz./25g cornflakes + 4fl.oz./
      ½ cup semi-skim milk   400mg
    1oz./25g oatmeal   10mg
    7oz./200g baked beans   1 gram

Zinc
Daily requirement
    adults and children   10mg
Sources
    6oz./160g ox liver   7.2mg
    1oz./25g cheese   1.1mg
    8fl.oz./1 cup milk   0.93mg

Personal Nutrition Notes

Use this space to note the nutritional values of your own favourite foods. Do they make a valuable contribution to your diet?

Personal Diet Notes

Copy this page to keep your own diet diary.

Monday
_____
_____
_____

Tuesday
_____
_____
_____

Wednesday
_____
_____
_____

Thursday
_____
_____
_____

Friday
_____
_____
_____

Saturday
_____
_____
_____

Sunday
_____
_____
_____

Index